HAL•LEONARD

UKULELE
PLAY-ALONG

AUDIO
ACCESS
INCLUDED

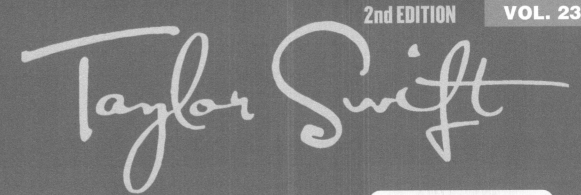

2nd EDITION

*Taylor Swift*

T0081807

# CONTENTS

*PLAYBACK+*
Speed • Pitch • Balance • Loop

To access audio visit:
**www.halleonard.com/mylibrary**

7754-9562-1140-7661

Photo © Big Machine Records, LLC

Ukulele performed by Chris Kringel

ISBN 978-1-4950-8969-5

HAL•LEONARD®
7777 W. BLUEMOUND RD. P.O. BOX 13819 MILWAUKEE, WI 53213

In Australia Contact:
**Hal Leonard Australia Pty. Ltd.**
4 Lentara Court
Cheltenham, Victoria, 3192 Australia
Email: ausadmin@halleonard.com.au

Visit Hal Leonard Online at
**www.halleonard.com**

# Blank Space

### Words and Music by Taylor Swift, Max Martin and Shellback

New mon-ey, suit and tie; I can read _ you like a mag-a-
Scream-ing, cry ing, per-fect storms; I can make _ all __ the ta-bles

zine. _ Ain't it fun-ny? Ru-mors fly, and I know _ you heard _ a-bout
turn. _ Rose _ gar-den filled with thorns; keep you sec - ond-guess - ing like,

me. So hey, let's be friends. I'm dy-ing to see how this one ends.
"Oh, my God, who is she?" I ___ get drunk on jeal-ous-y. But

N.C.

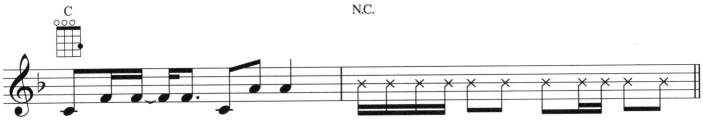

Grab your pass - port and my hand. I can make the bad guys good for a week-end.
you'll come back _ each time you leave, 'cause, dar-ling, I'm a night-mare dressed like a day-dream.

𝄋 **Chorus**

So it's gon-na be for-ev - er, or it's gon-na go down in flames. _

You can tell me when it's o - ver, mm, if the high was worth the pain. _

3

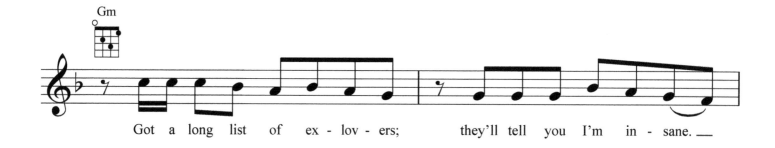

Got a long list of ex - lov - ers; they'll tell you I'm in - sane. __

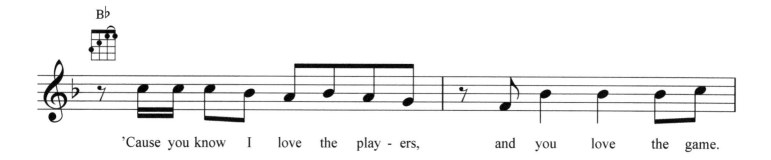

'Cause you know I love the play - ers, and you love the game.

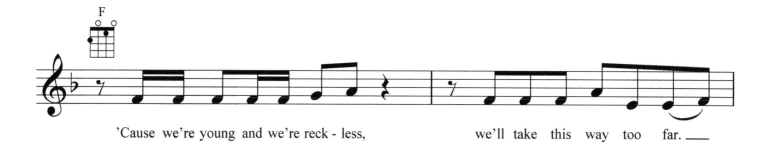

'Cause we're young and we're reck - less, we'll take this way too far. __

It - 'll leave you breath - less, mm, or with a nas - ty scar. __

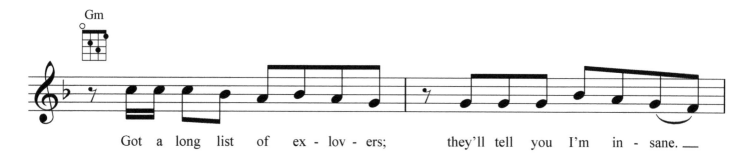

Got a long list of ex - lov - ers; they'll tell you I'm in - sane. __

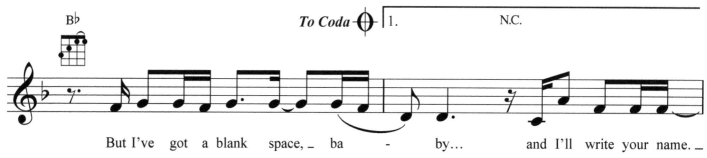

But I've got a blank space, __ ba - by... and I'll write your name. __

4

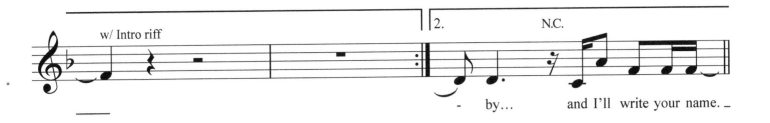

- by... and I'll write your name. ___

## Bridge

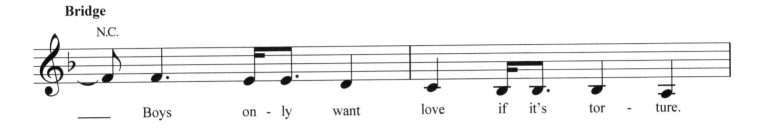

___ Boys on - ly want love if it's tor - ture.

Don't say I did - n't, say I did - n't warn ya.

Boys on - ly want love if it's tor - ture.

*D.S. al Coda*

Don't say I did - n't, say I did - n't warn ya.

**Coda**

- by... and I'll write your name. ___

# I Knew You Were Trouble

Words and Music by Taylor Swift, Shellback and Max Martin

First note

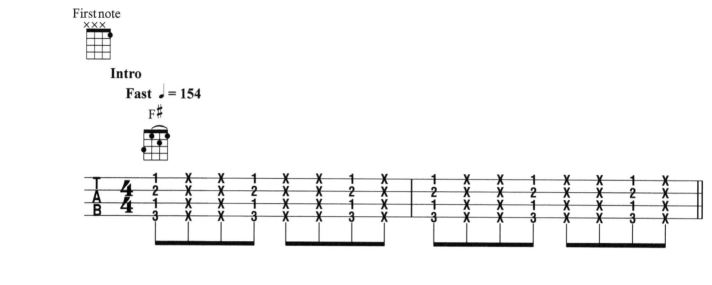

1. Once up - on a time, a few mis - takes a - go,
2. No a - pol - o - gies, he'll nev - er see you cry. Pre -

I was in your sights, you got me a - lone. You
tends he does - n't know that he's the rea - son why you're

found _____ me, you found _____ me, you
drown - ing, you're drown - ing, you're

found _____ me, ee, ee, ee, ee. I
drown - ing, ing, ing, ing, ing. And I

guess you did-n't care, and I guess I liked that. And
heard you moved \_ on, from \_ whis-pers on the street. A

when I fell hard, you took a step back with -
new notch in your belt is all I'll ev - er be. And

out _____ me, with - out _____ me, with -
now _____ I see, now _____ I see,

out _____ me, ee, ee, ee, ee. _____
now _____ I see, ee, ee, ee, ee. _____

**Pre-Chorus**

And he's long _____ gone when he's next \_
He was long _____ gone when he met \_

to ___ me, and I re - a - lize ___
me, and I re - a - lize ___

the blame is on ___ me. ___
the joke is on ___ me. ___ 'Cause

𝄋 Chorus

I knew you were trou-ble when you walked in, _____ so

shame on me now. ___ Flew me to plac - es I'd nev - er been ___

_____ till you put me down. Oh, I knew you were

trou - ble when you walked in, _____ so

8

that you nev - er loved me or her, _____ or

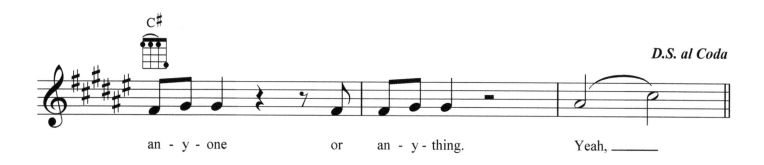

*D.S. al Coda*

an - y - one or an - y - thing. Yeah, _____

**Coda**  **Outro**

trou-ble, trou-ble. I knew you were trou-ble when you walked in. ___

___ Trou-ble, trou - ble, trou - ble. I knew you were

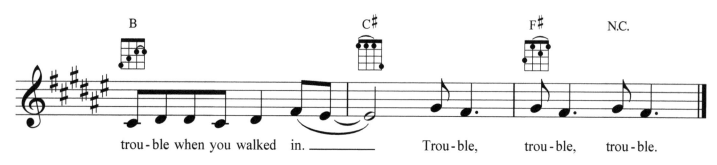

trou-ble when you walked in. _____ Trou-ble, trou-ble, trou - ble.

# Mean

**Words and Music by Taylor Swift**

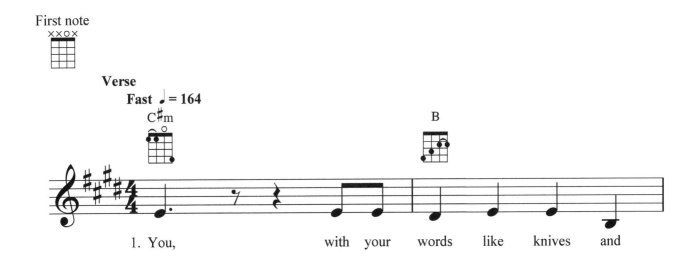

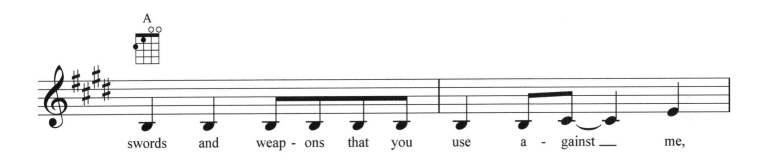

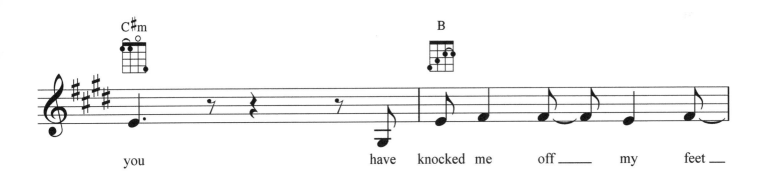

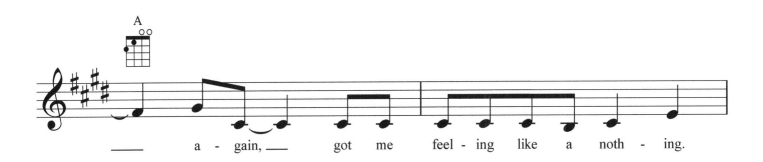

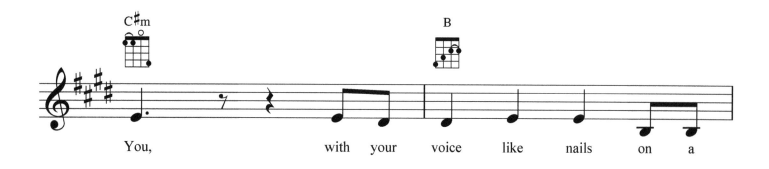

You,      with your voice like nails on a

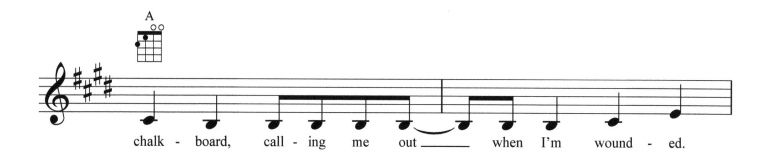

chalk - board, call - ing me out _____ when I'm wound - ed.

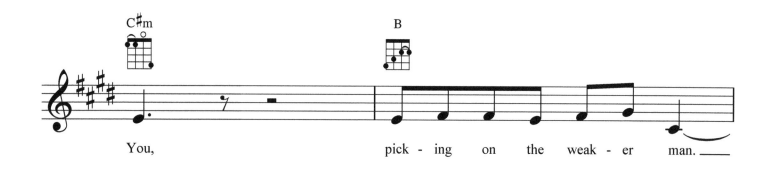

You,      pick - ing on the weak - er man. _____

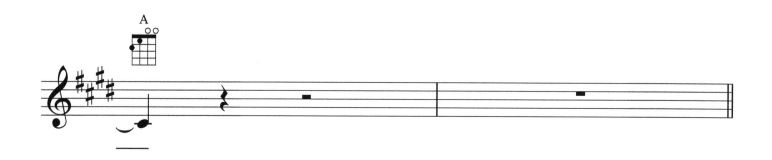

**Pre-Chorus**

Well, you can take me down _____

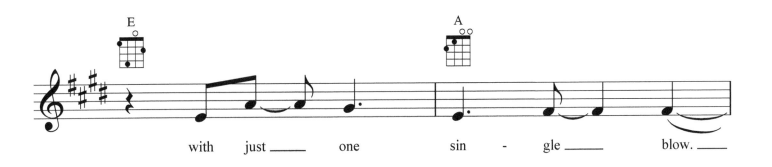

with just ____ one sin - gle ____ blow. ____

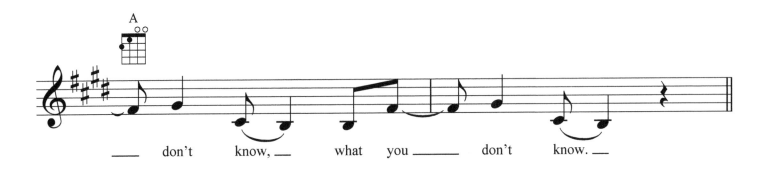

But you ____

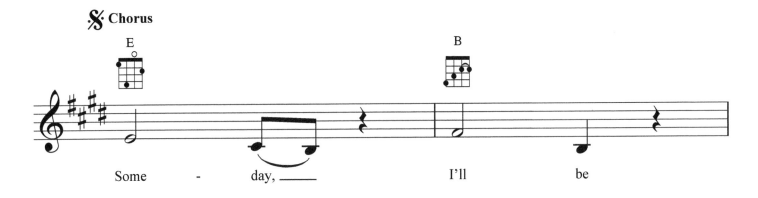

____ don't know, ____ what you ____ don't know. ____

%: Chorus

Some - day, ____ I'll be

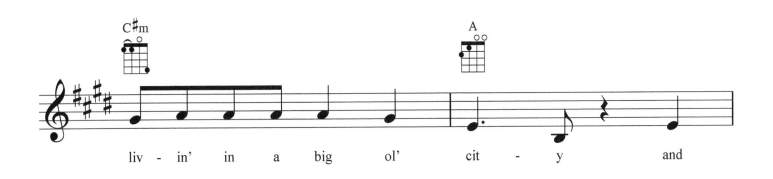

liv - in' in a big ol' cit - y and

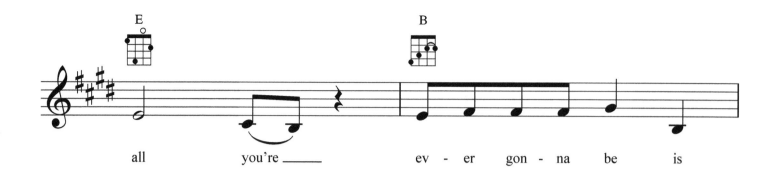

all you're _____ ev - er gon - na be is

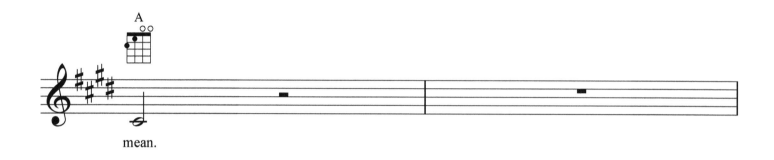

mean.

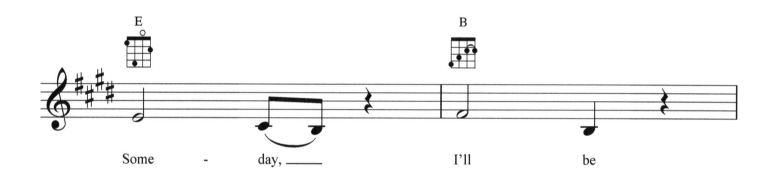

Some - day, _____ I'll be

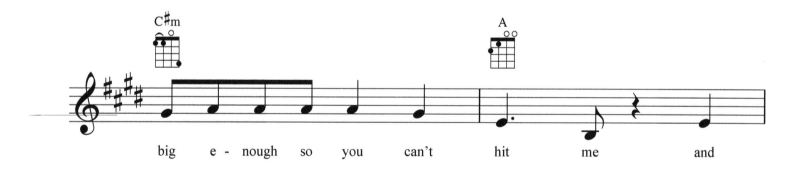

big e - nough so you can't hit me and

*To Coda* ⊕

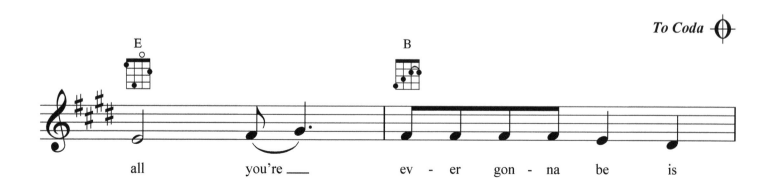

all you're _____ ev - er gon - na be is

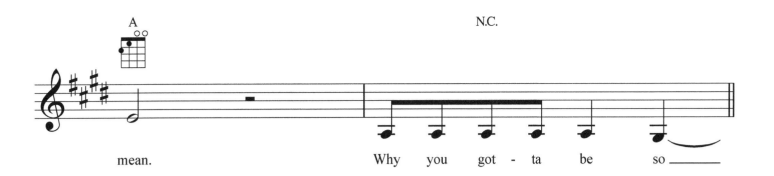

mean.                    Why    you    got - ta    be    so _____

**Interlude**

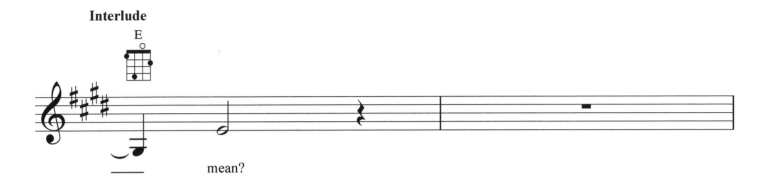

_____    mean?

**Verse**

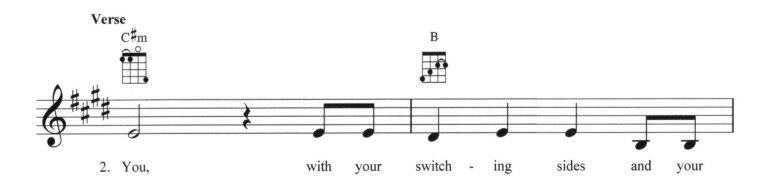

2. You,                    with    your    switch - ing    sides    and    your

wild - fire    lies    and    your    hu - mil - i - a - tion,

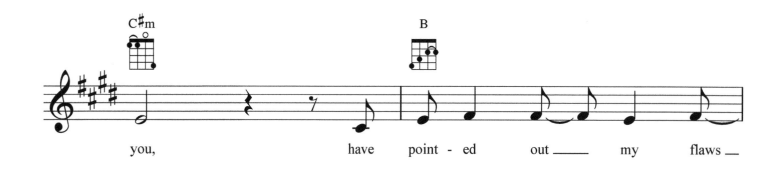

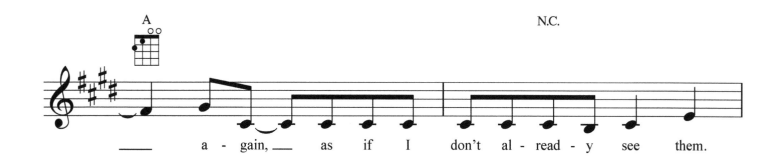

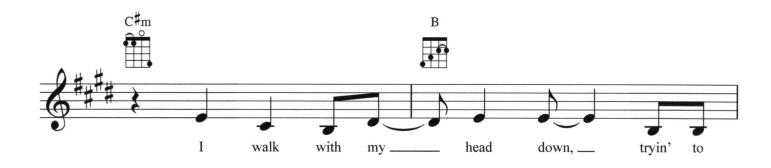

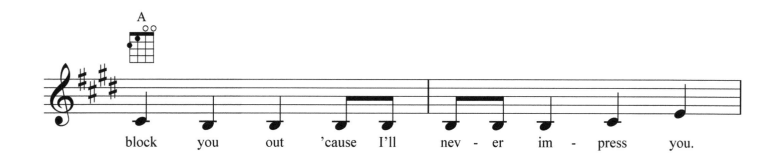

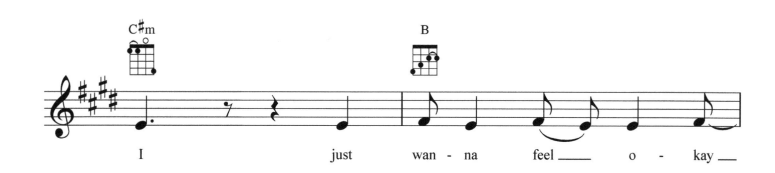

a - gain. \_\_\_\_

**Pre-Chorus**

I bet you got pushed a - round, _____

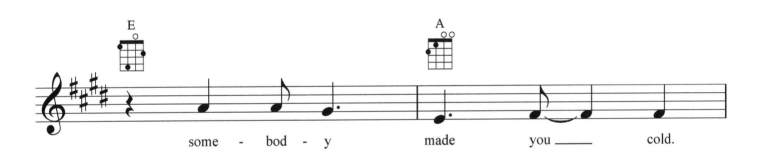

some - bod - y made you \_\_\_\_ cold.

But the cy - cle ends \_\_\_\_ right now, _____ 'cause

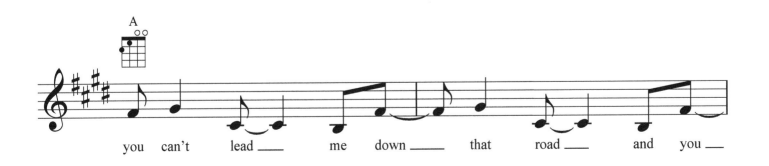

you can't lead \_\_\_\_ me down \_\_\_\_ that road \_\_\_\_ and you \_\_\_\_

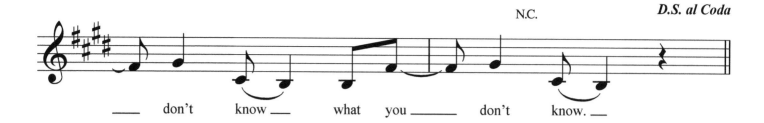

N.C.

\_\_ don't    know \_\_    what    you \_\_\_\_    don't      know. \_\_

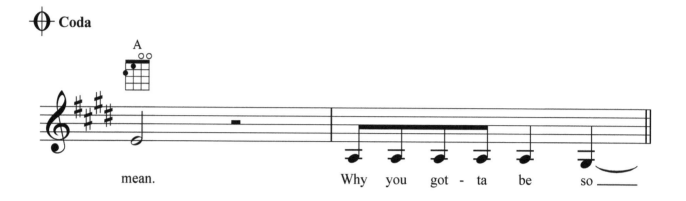

**Coda**

A

mean.        Why    you    got - ta    be    so \_\_

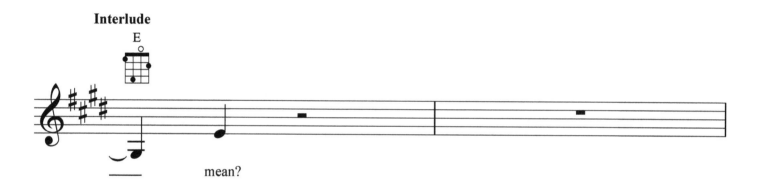

**Interlude**

E

\_\_        mean?

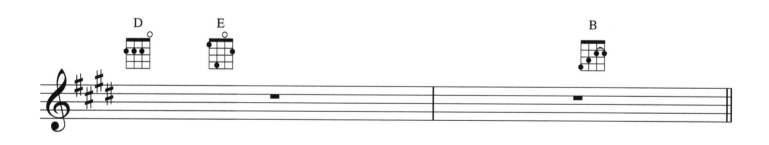

D        E                                                    B

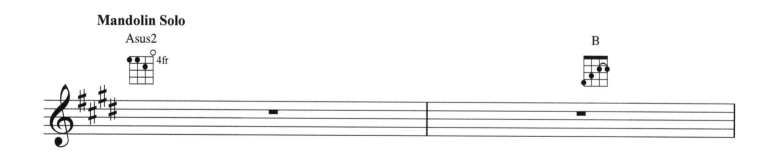

**Mandolin Solo**

Asus2                                                        B

And    I       can ____

**Bridge**

see   you   years ____ from   now _____ in   a   bar, ____

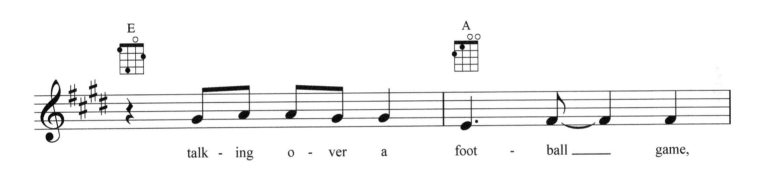

talk - ing   o - ver   a     foot - ball ____ game,

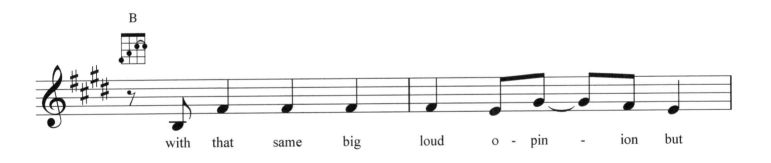

with   that   same   big   loud   o - pin - ion   but

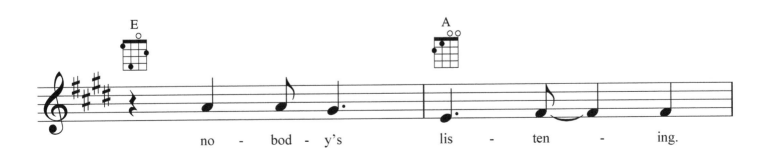

no - bod - y's    lis - ten - ing.

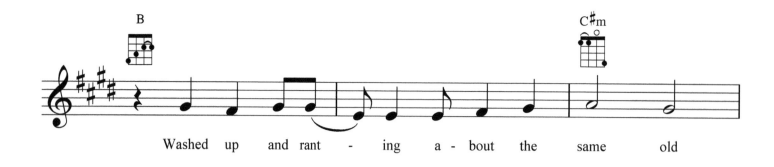

Washed up and rant - ing a - bout the same old

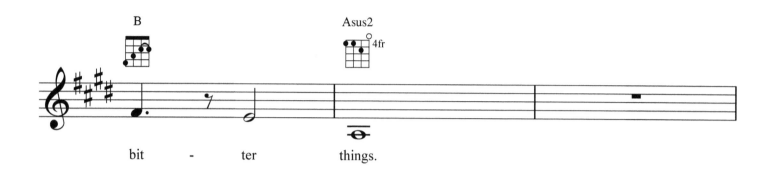

bit - ter things.

Drunk and grum - blin' on _____ a - bout _____ how

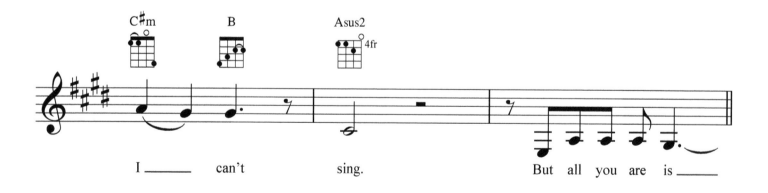

I _____ can't sing. But all you are is _____

**Interlude**

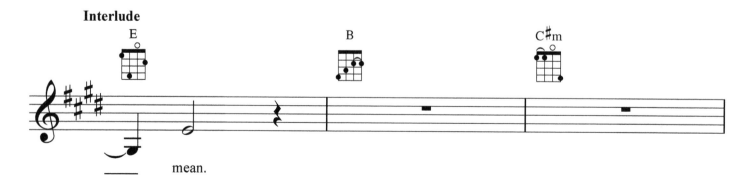

_____ mean.

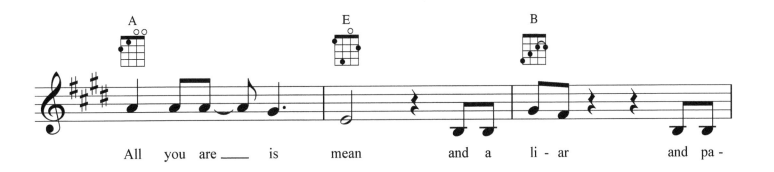

All you are ___ is mean and a li - ar and pa -

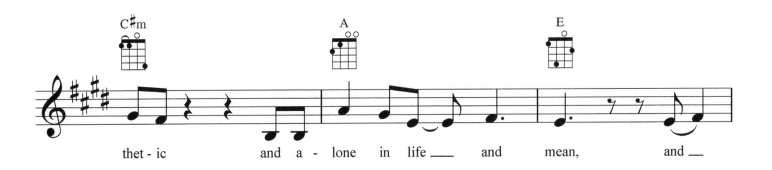

thet - ic and a - lone in life ___ and mean, and ___

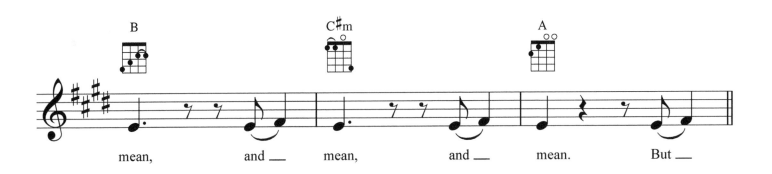

mean, and ___ mean, and ___ mean. But ___

**Chorus**

some - day, ___ I'll be liv - in' in a big ol'

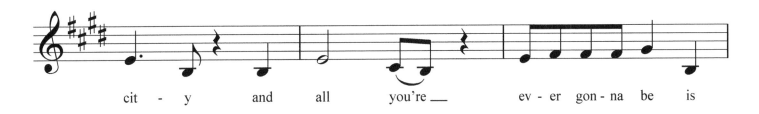

cit - y and all you're ___ ev - er gon - na be is

mean.       Yeah! _____      Some - day, \_\_

I'll \_\_   be      big e -nough so you can't   hit   me   and

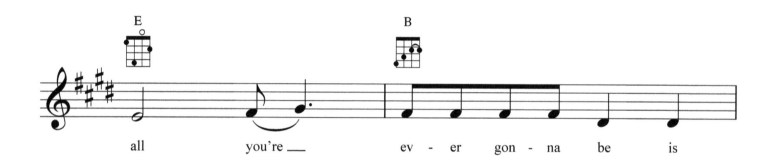

all      you're \_\_     ev - er gon - na be   is

**Chorus**

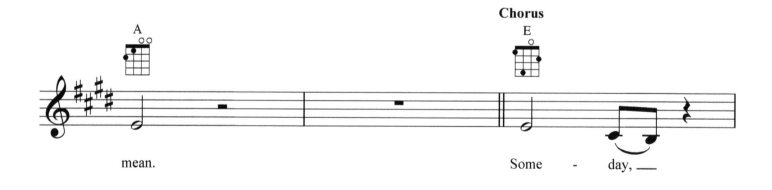

mean.         Some - day, \_\_

I'll   be      liv - in' in a big ol' cit - y   and

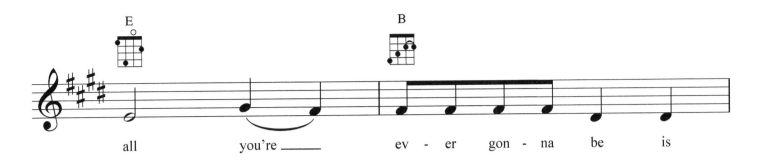

all      you're _____    ev - er   gon - na   be   is

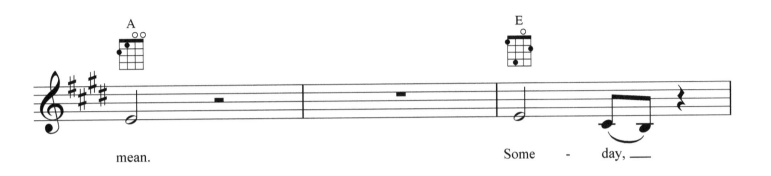

mean.                            Some  -  day, _____

I'll _____ be     big   e - nough so   you   can't   hit   me     and

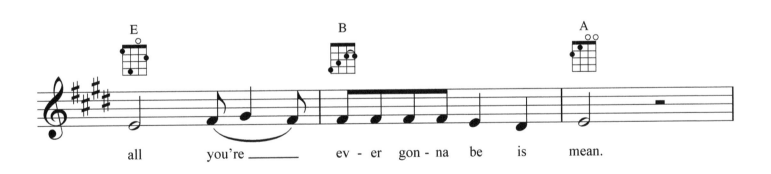

all      you're _____    ev - er   gon - na   be   is   mean.

Why   you   got - ta   be   so _____   mean?

# Love Story

**Words and Music by Taylor Swift**

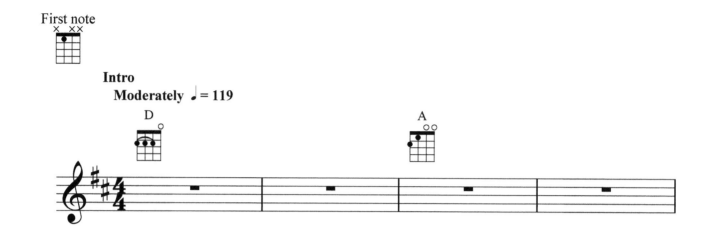

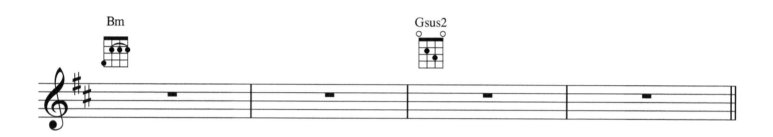

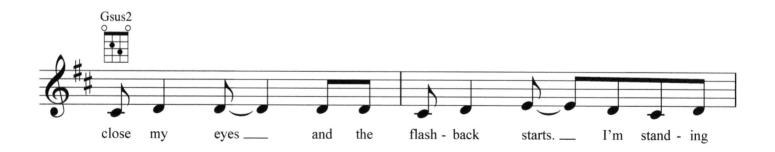

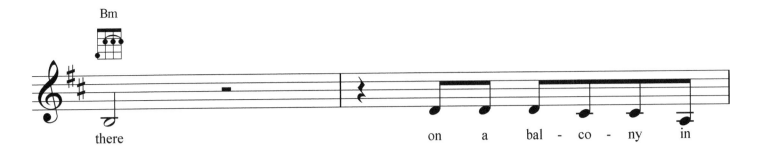

**Bm**

there                                       on    a    bal - co - ny    in

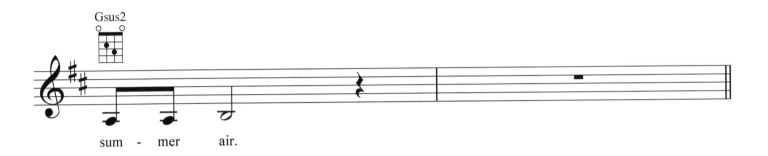

**Gsus2**

sum - mer   air.

**Verse**
**D**

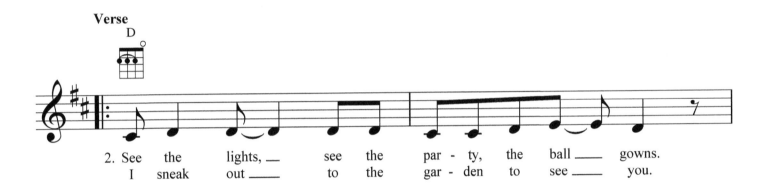

2. See    the     lights, __    see    the    par - ty,    the    ball __    gowns.
   I   sneak    out __    to    the    gar - den    to    see __    you.

**G**

See    you      make __    your    way    through    the    crowd __    and    say    hel -
We    keep      qui - et   'cause we're    dead    if    they    knew. __    So    close    your

**Bm**

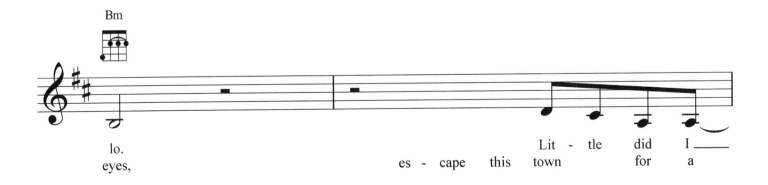

lo.                                       Lit - tle    did    I __
eyes,                       es - cape    this    town          for    a

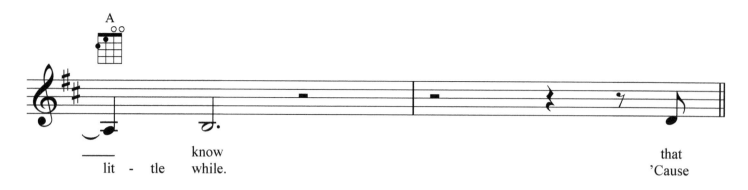

know
lit - tle while.
that
'Cause

**Pre-Chorus**

you were Ro - me - o. You were throw - ing peb - bles and my
you were Ro - me - o. I was a scar - let let - ter and my

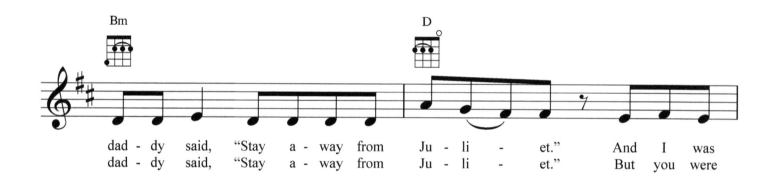

dad - dy said, "Stay a - way from Ju - li - et." And I was
dad - dy said, "Stay a - way from Ju - li - et." But you were

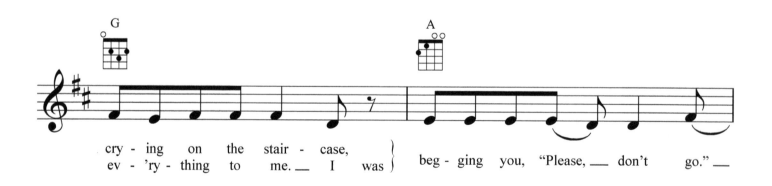

cry - ing on the stair - case, I was
ev - 'ry - thing to me. I was beg - ging you, "Please, don't go."

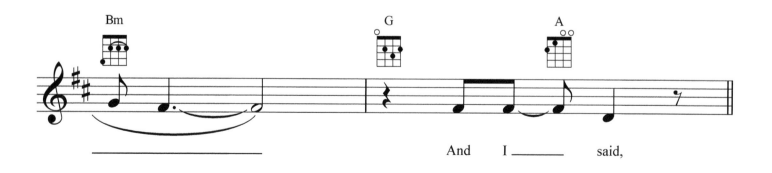

And I said,

**Chorus**

"Ro - me - o, take ___ me some - where we can be a - lone.

I'll be wait - ing; all there's left to do is run.

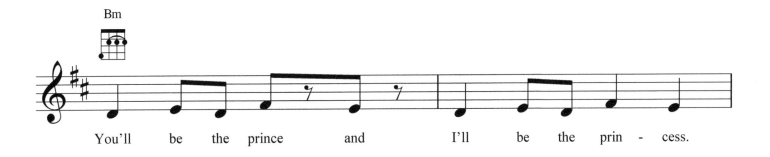

You'll be the prince and I'll be the prin - cess.

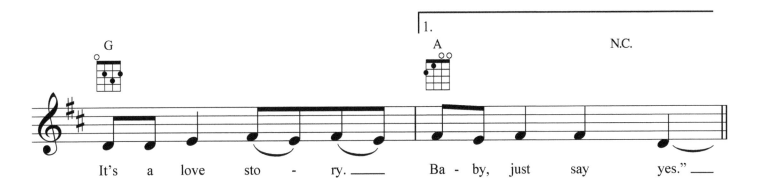

It's a love sto - ry. ___ Ba - by, just say yes." ___

**Interlude**

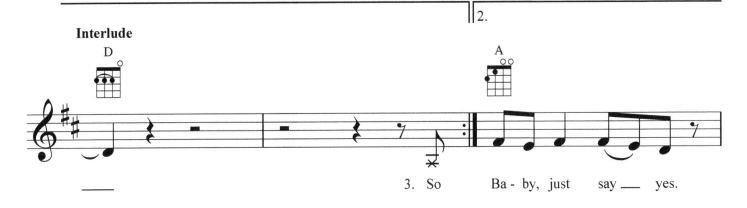

3. So Ba - by, just say ___ yes.

Ro - me - o, save ___ me. They're try'n' to tell me how to feel.

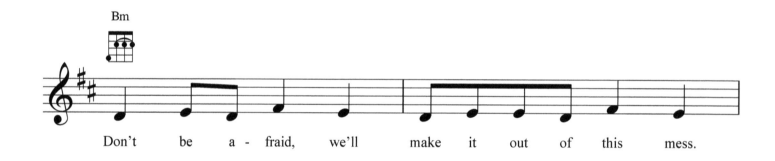

This love is dif - fi - cult, but it's, uh, real. _____

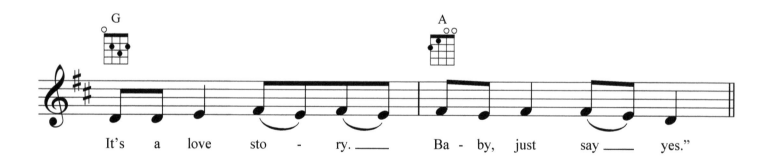

Don't be a - fraid, we'll make it out of this mess.

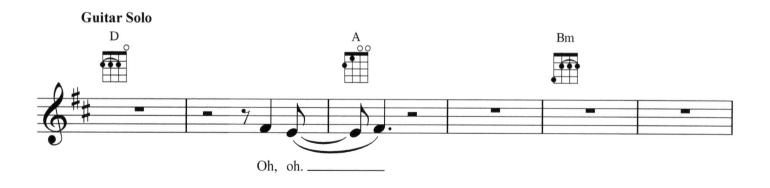

It's a love sto - ry. ___ Ba - by, just say ___ yes."

**Guitar Solo**

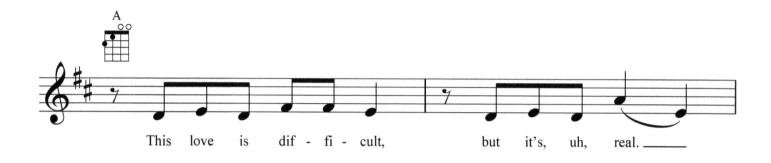

Oh, oh. _____

I got tired of wait - ing, ____

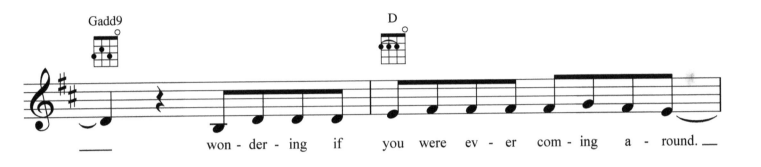

____ won - der - ing if you were ev - er com - ing a - round. __

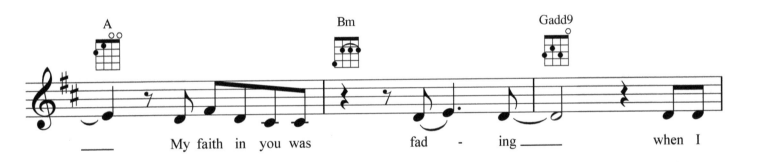

____ My faith in you was fad - ing ____ when I

**End half-time feel**

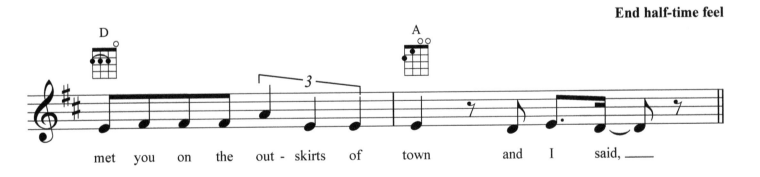

met you on the out - skirts of town and I said, ____

**Chorus**

"Ro - me - o, save __ me. I've been feel - ing so a - lone."

I keep wait - ing for you, but you nev - er come. Is

this in my head? I don't know what to think. He ____

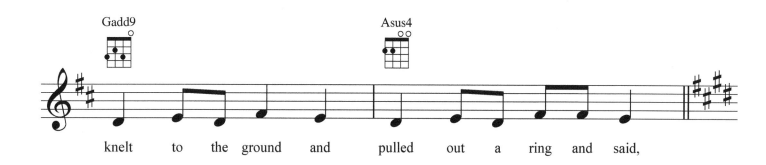

knelt to the ground and pulled out a ring and said,

**Chorus**

"Mar - ry me, Ju - li - et. You'll nev - er have to be a - lone.

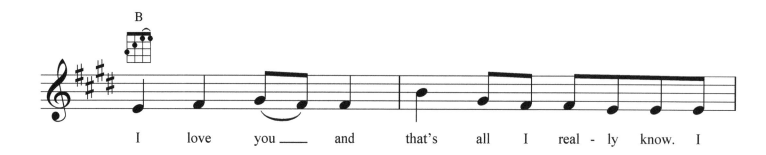

I love you ____ and that's all I real - ly know. I

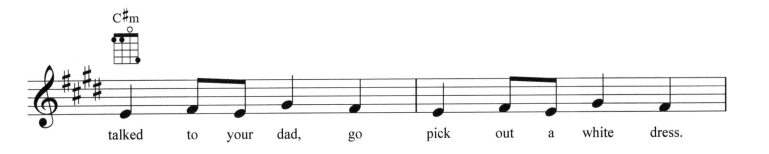

talked    to    your    dad,    go    pick    out    a    white    dress.

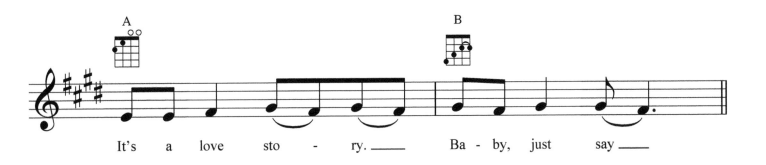

It's    a    love    sto - ry. \_\_\_    Ba - by,    just    say \_\_\_

**Outro**

yes." \_       Oh,    oh,    oh. _____

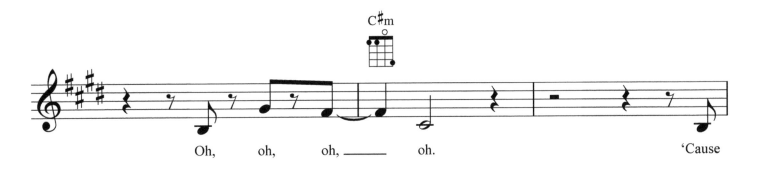

Oh,    oh,    oh, \_\_\_    oh.       'Cause

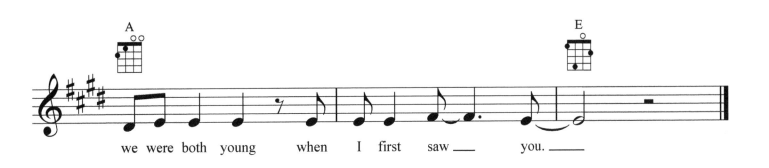

we   were   both   young    when    I    first    saw \_\_\_    you. \_\_\_

# Safe & Sound

from THE HUNGER GAMES

**Words and Music by Taylor Swift, T-Bone Burnett, John Paul White and Joy Williams**

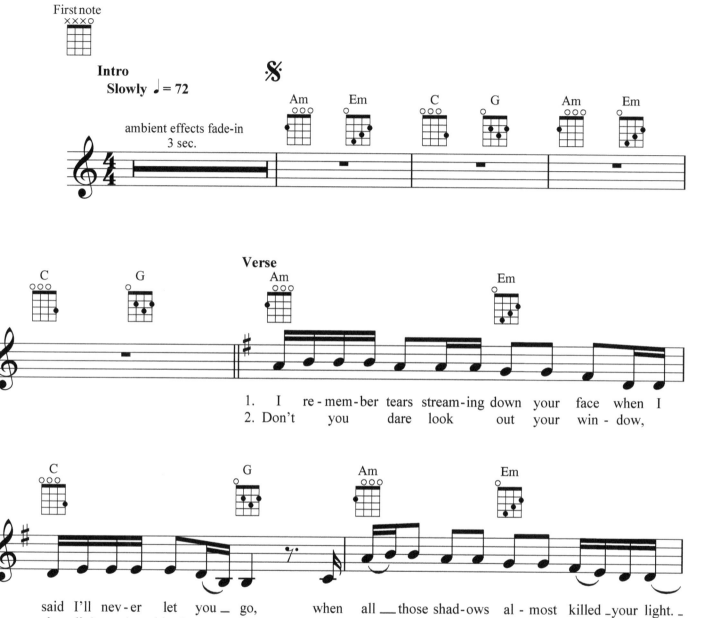

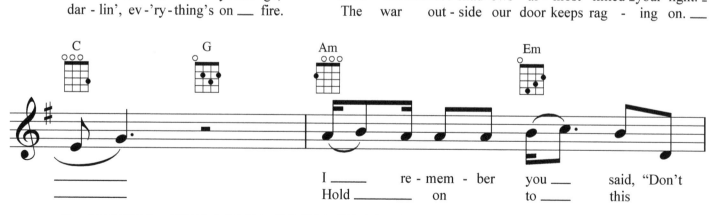

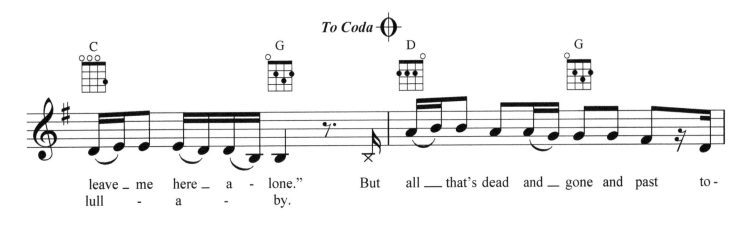

*To Coda* ⊕

leave _ me here a - lone." But all __ that's dead and __ gone and past to -
lull - a - by.

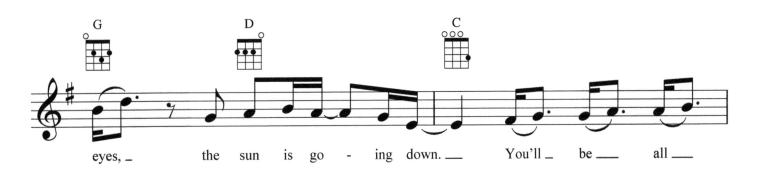

night. _____ Just __ close __ your __

**Chorus**

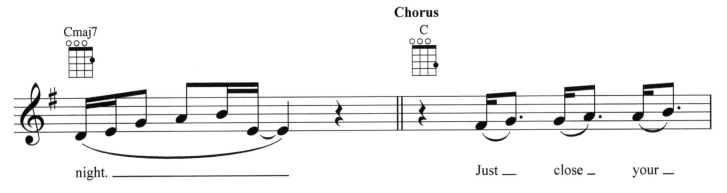

eyes, _ the sun is go - ing down. __ You'll _ be __ all __

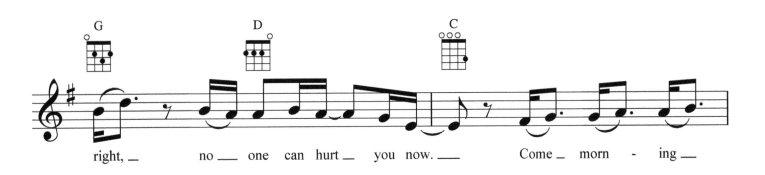

right, _ no __ one can hurt _ you now. __ Come _ morn - ing _

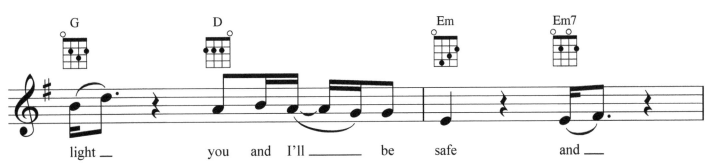

light _ you and I'll __ be safe and __

**33**

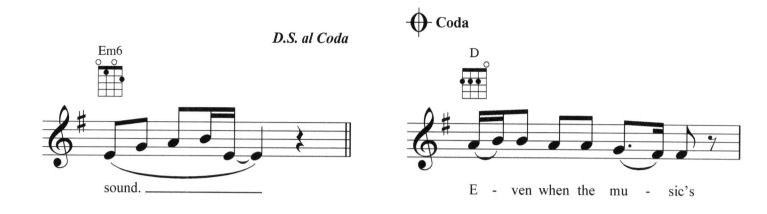

*D.S. al Coda*

**⊕ Coda**

Em6

sound. _____

D

E - ven when the mu - sic's

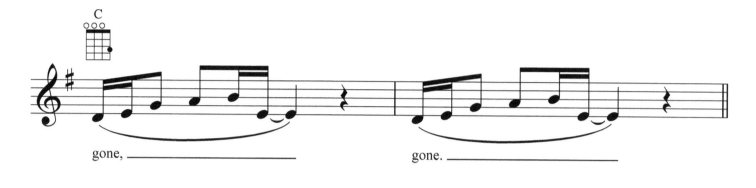

C

gone, _____

gone. _____

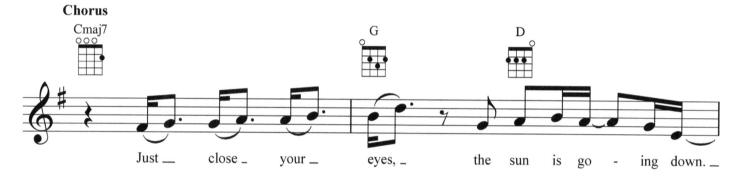

**Chorus**

Cmaj7

G

D

Just __ close __ your __ eyes, __ the sun is go - ing down. __

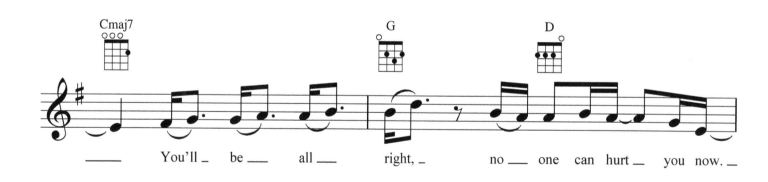

Cmaj7

G

D

__ You'll __ be __ all __ right, __ no __ one can hurt __ you now. __

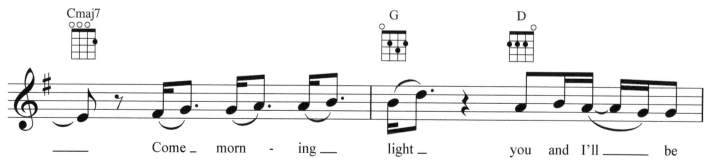

Cmaj7

G

D

__ Come __ morn - ing __ light __ you and I'll _____ be

34

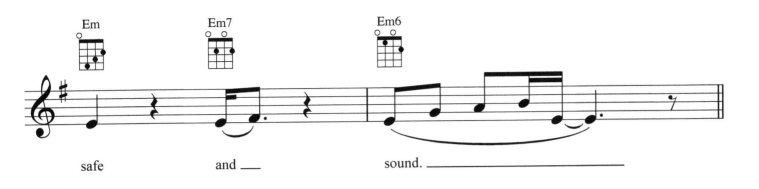

safe      and ___      sound. _____

**Bridge**

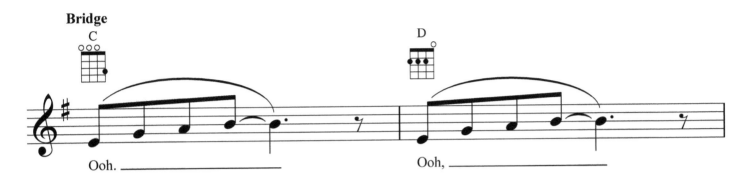

Ooh. _____      Ooh, _____

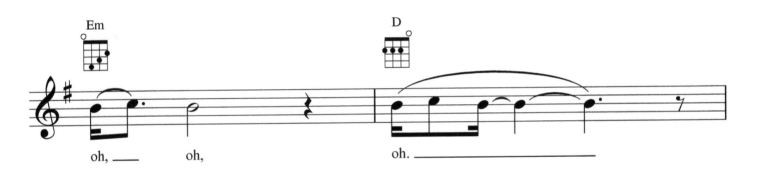

oh, ___    oh,      oh. _____

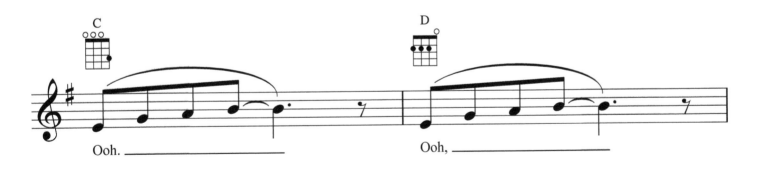

Ooh. _____      Ooh, _____

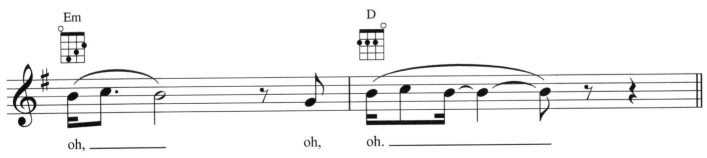

oh, _____      oh,    oh. _____

**Chorus**

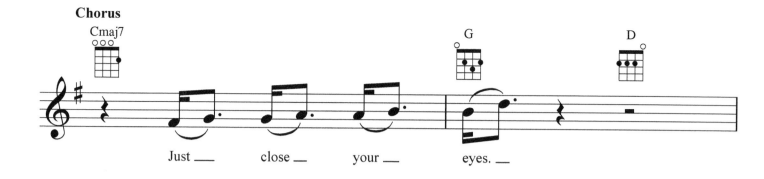

Just \_\_\_ close \_\_\_ your \_\_\_ eyes. \_\_\_

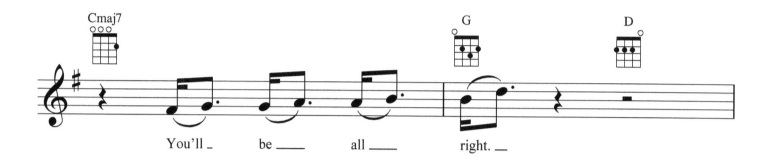

You'll \_ be \_\_\_ all \_\_\_ right. \_\_\_

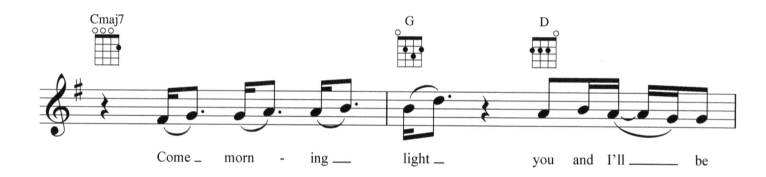

Come \_ morn - ing \_\_\_ light \_ you and I'll \_\_\_ be

safe and \_\_\_ sound. _____ Ooh, _____

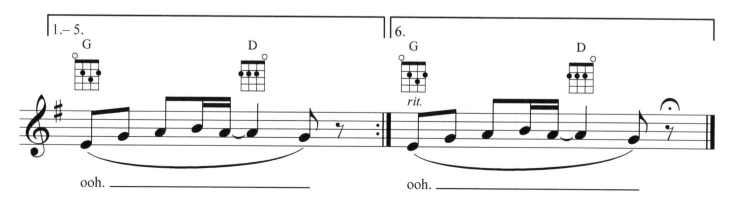

1. – 5.

ooh. _____

6.

ooh. _____

# White Horse

**Words and Music by Taylor Swift and Liz Rose**

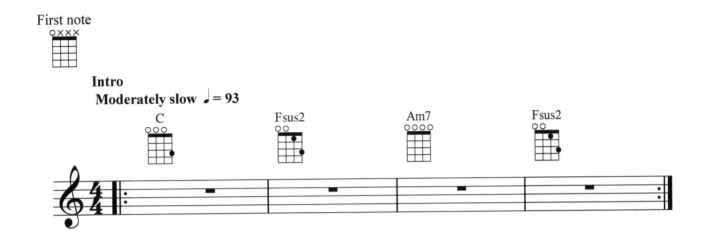

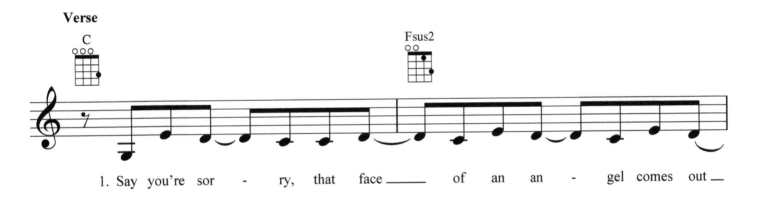

1. Say you're sor - ry, that face ___ of an an - gel comes out ___ ___ just when you need it to

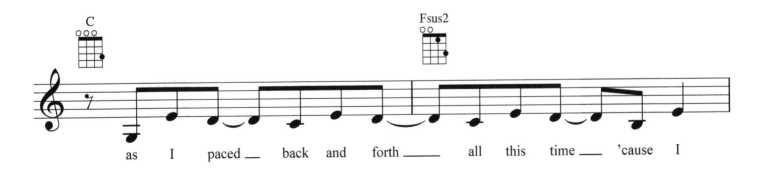

as I paced ___ back and forth ___ all this time ___ 'cause I

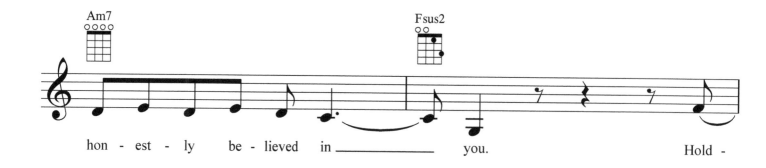

hon - est - ly be - lieved in _____ you.                                        Hold -

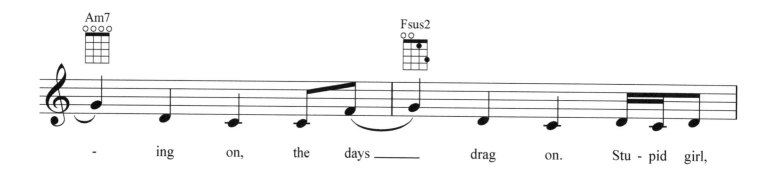

- ing on, the days _____ drag on.     Stu - pid girl,

I should - 've known,     I should - 've known \_\_\_     that I'm not a prin -

**𝄉 Chorus**

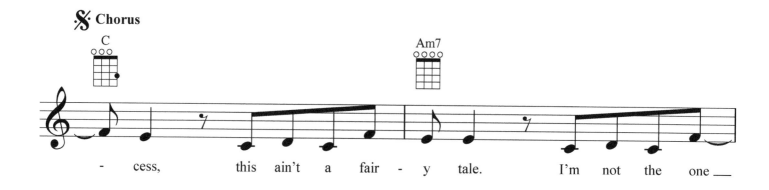

- cess,     this ain't a fair - y tale.     I'm not the one \_\_\_

\_\_\_\_\_ you'll sweep off her feet,     lead her up the stair - well. This ain't

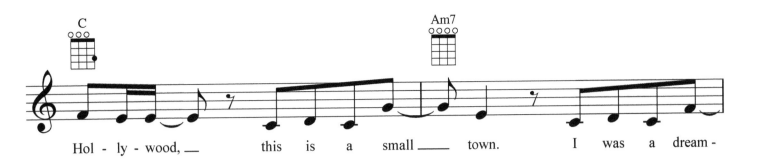

Hol - ly - wood, — this is a small ___ town. I was a dream -

*To Coda* ⊕

- er be - fore you went and let me down. ___ Now it's too ___

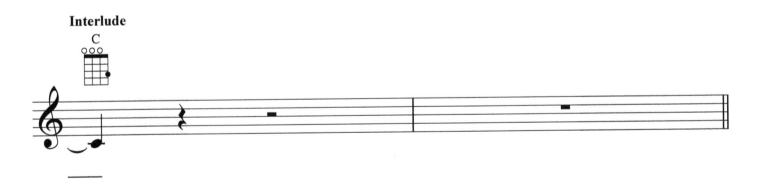

___ late for you ___ and your white ___ horse to come a - round. ___

**Interlude**

**Verse**

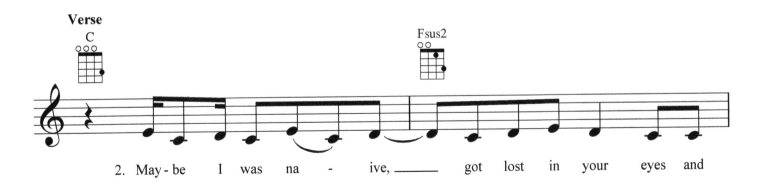

2. May - be I was na - ive, ___ got lost in your eyes and

nev - er real - ly had a chance.

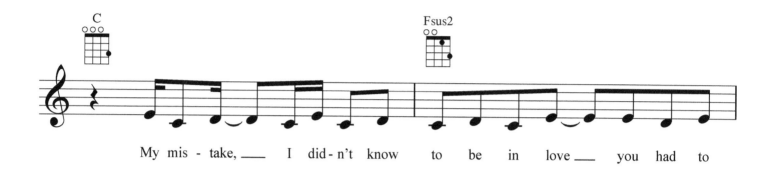

My mis - take, ___ I did - n't know to be in love ___ you had to

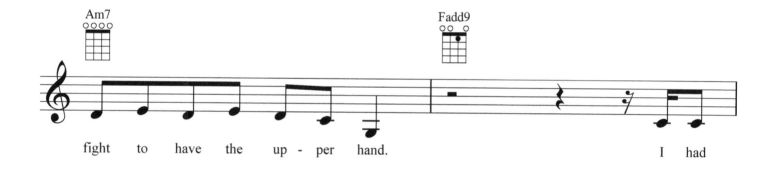

fight to have the up - per hand. I had

*D.S. al Coda*

so man - y dreams a - bout you ___ and me. ___ Hap - py end -

- ings, now ___ I know ___ that I'm not a prin -

**Coda**

_____ late for you _____ and your white _____ horse to come a - round. _____

**Interlude**

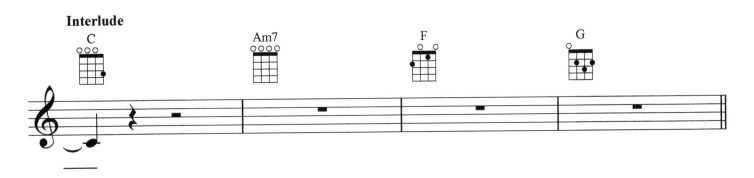

**Bridge**

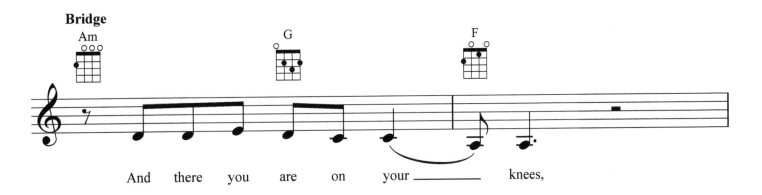

And there you are on your _____ knees,

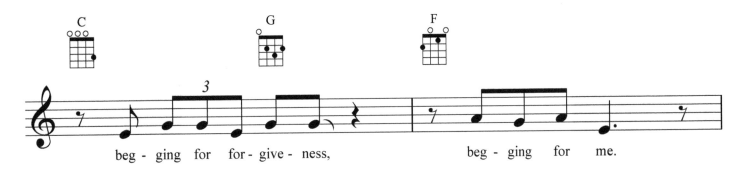

beg - ging for for - give - ness, beg - ging for me.

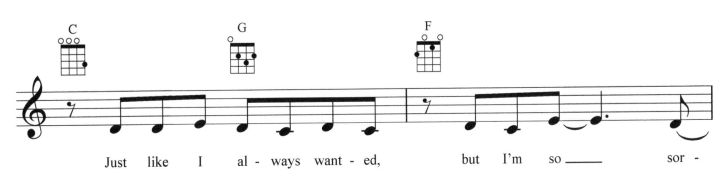

Just like I al - ways want - ed, but I'm so _____ sor -

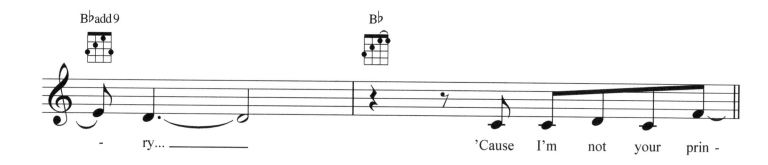

-ry... \_\_\_\_\_ 'Cause I'm not your prin -

**Chorus**

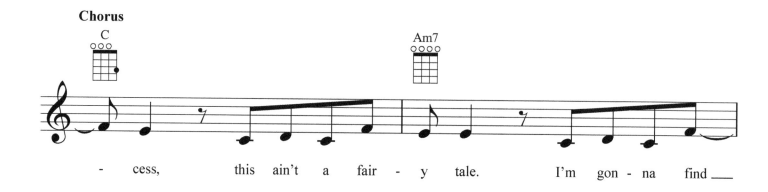

- cess, this ain't a fair - y tale. I'm gon - na find \_\_\_

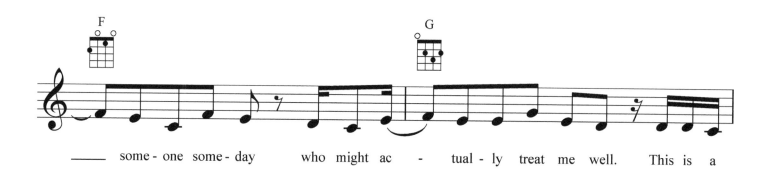

\_\_\_\_ some - one some - day who might ac - tual - ly treat me well. This is a

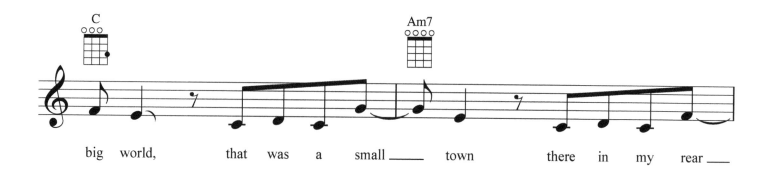

big world, that was a small \_\_\_ town there in my rear \_\_\_

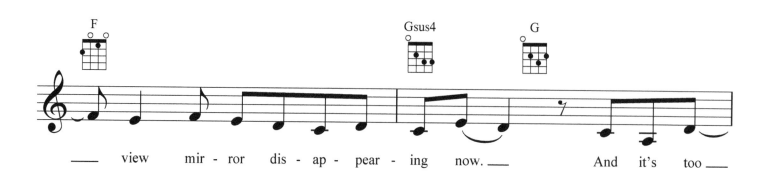

\_\_\_ view mir - ror dis - ap - pear - ing now. \_\_\_ And it's too \_\_\_

late for you ___ and your white ___ horse, now it's too ___

late for you ___ and your white ___ horse to catch me ___

**Outro**

___ now. Oh, ___ whoa, _____ whoa, ___ whoa. _____

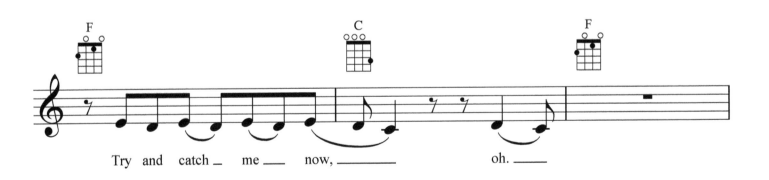

Try and catch ___ me ___ now, _____ oh. _____

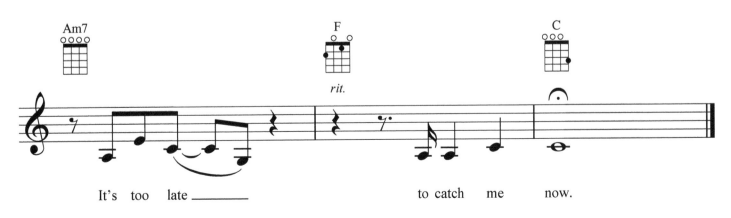

It's too late _____ to catch me now.

# Shake It Off

**Words and Music by Taylor Swift, Max Martin and Shellback**

mm.    I    go    on    too    man - y    dates,
mm.    I'm    danc - ing    on    my    own;

but    I    can't    make    'em    stay.
I    make    the    moves    up    as    I    go.

At    least,    that's    what    peo - ple    say, _____ mm,
And    that's    what    they    don't    know, _____ mm,

mm.    That's    what    peo - ple    say, _____ mm,
mm.    That's    what    they    don't    know, _____ mm,

**Pre-Chorus**

mm. But    I    keep    cruis - ing;    can't    stop, won't    stop
mm. But    I    keep    cruis - ing;    can't    stop, won't    stop

mov - ing. }
groov - ing. }    It's    like    I    got    this    mu - sic

in my mind say - ing, "It's gon - na be al - right." ___
*Play 1st time only

𝄋 **Chorus**

'Cause the play - ers gon - na play, play,

play, play, play, and the hat - ers gon - na hate, hate,

hate, hate, hate. Ba - by, I'm just gon - na shake, shake,

shake, shake, shake. ___ A, shake it off, a, shake it

off. Heart - break - ers gon - na break, break,
(Ooh, _____ ooh!)

break,     break,     break,     and     the     fak - ers   gon - na   fake,     fake,

fake,     fake,     fake.     Ba - by,     I'm     just    gon - na   shake,     shake,

*To Coda*

shake,     shake,     shake.     A,     shake     it     off,     a,     shake    it

1.

off.     2. I     nev - er    miss    a
(Ooh, _____ ooh!)

2.

off. (Ooh, _____ ooh!)

**Bridge**

Shake     it     off,     a,     shake     it     off.     I,     I,     a,

shake     it     off,     a,     shake     it     off.     I,     I,     a,

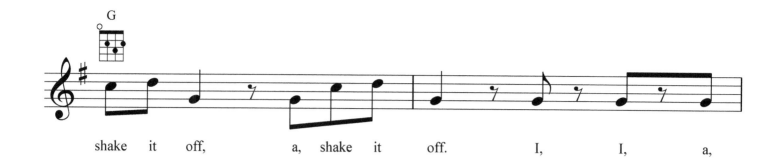

shake it off,    a, shake it off.    I,    I,    a,

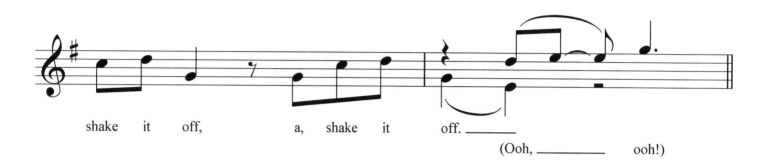

shake it off,    a, shake it off. _____

(Ooh, _____ ooh!)

**Interlude**

N.C.

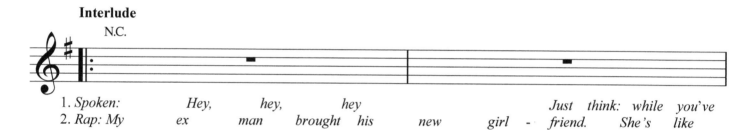

1. *Spoken:*     Hey,    hey,    hey       *Just think: while you've*
2. *Rap: My*    ex    man    brought his    new    girl - friend. She's    like

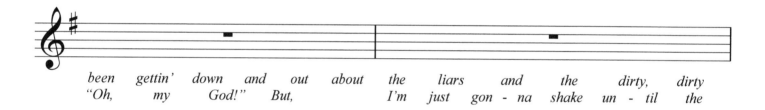

been gettin' down and out about the liars and the dirty, dirty
*"Oh, my God!" But, I'm just gon - na shake un - til the*

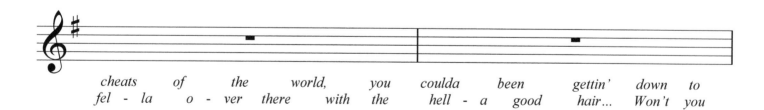

cheats of the world, you coulda been gettin' down to
*fel - la o - ver there with the hell - a good hair... Won't you*

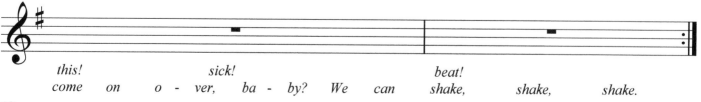

this!      sick!      beat!
come on o - ver, ba - by? We can shake, shake, shake.

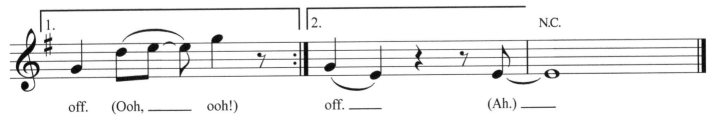

# Teardrops on My Guitar

Words and Music by Taylor Swift and Liz Rose

First note

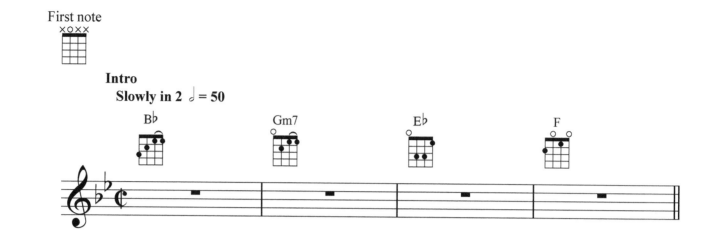

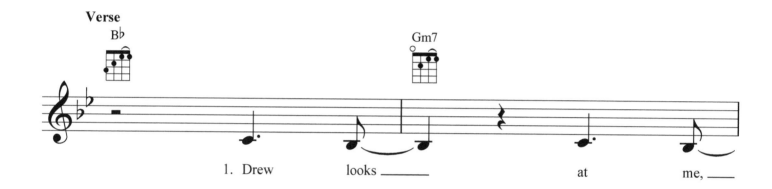

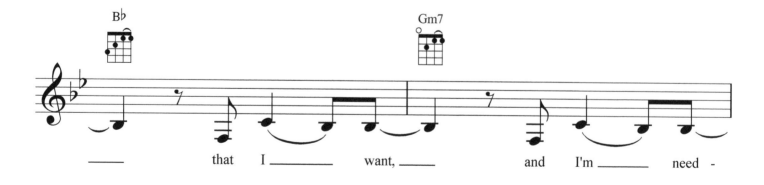

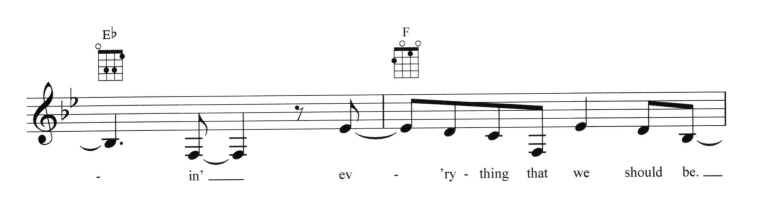

-in' _____ ev - 'ry - thing that we should be. _____

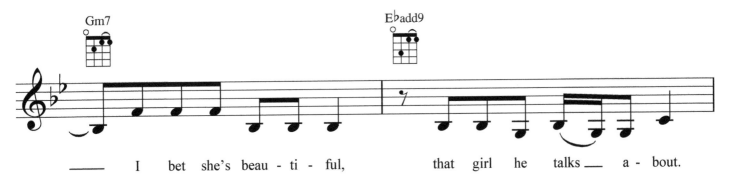

_____ I bet she's beau - ti - ful, that girl he talks _____ a - bout.

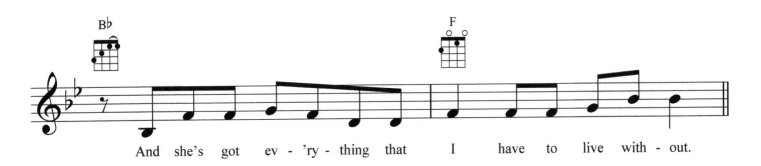

And she's got ev - 'ry - thing that I have to live with - out.

**Verse**

2. Drew talks _____ to me, _____
3. Drew walks _____ by me, _____

_____ I laugh _____ 'cause it's just so fun - ny _____
_____ can _____ he tell that I can't breathe? _____

the on - ly thing that keeps me wish - in' on a wish - in' star.

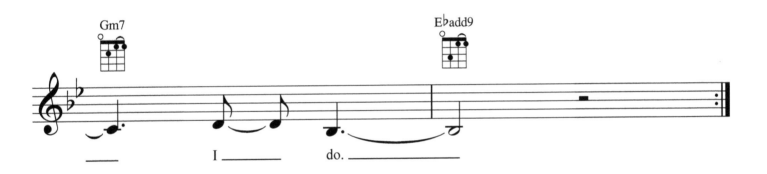

He's the song in the car I keep sing - in', don't know why ___

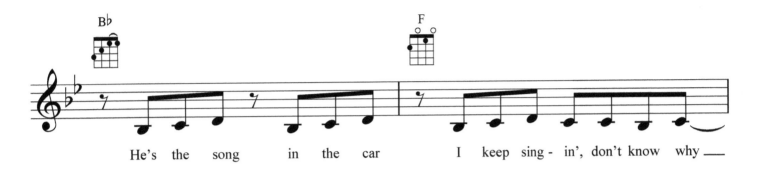

___ I _____ do. _____

**Interlude**

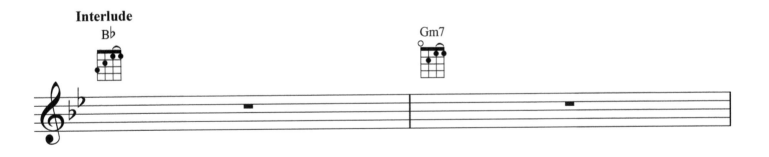

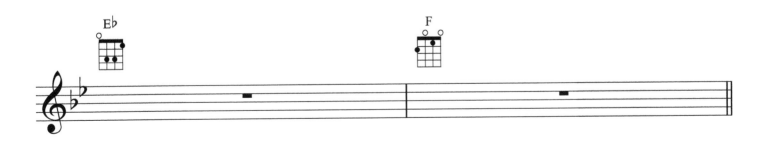

**Bridge**

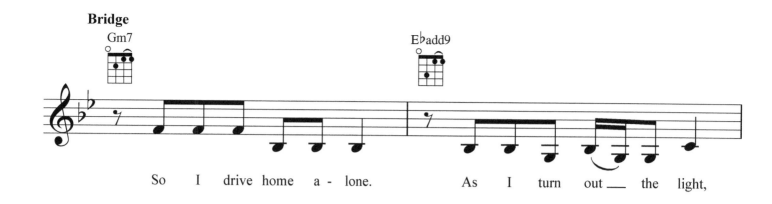

So I drive home a - lone. As I turn out ___ the light,

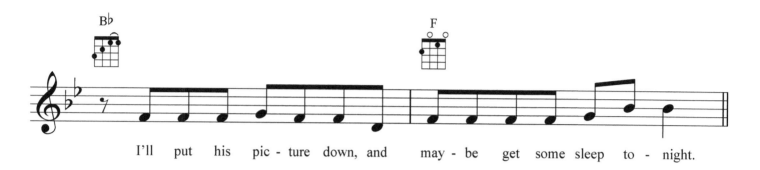

I'll put his pic - ture down, and may - be get some sleep to - night.

**Chorus**

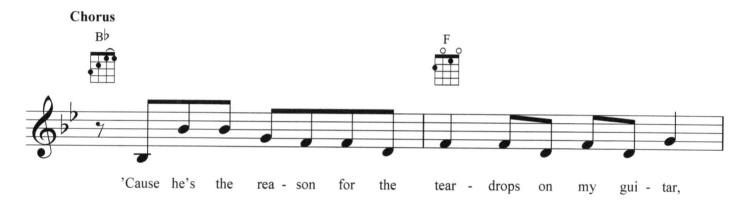

'Cause he's the rea - son for the tear - drops on my gui - tar,

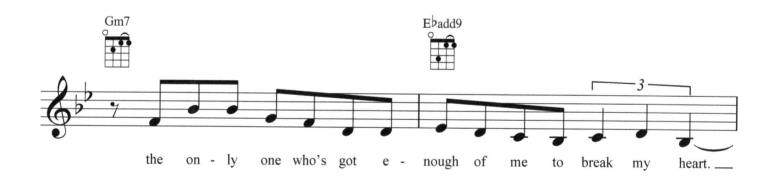

the on - ly one who's got e - nough of me to break my heart. ___

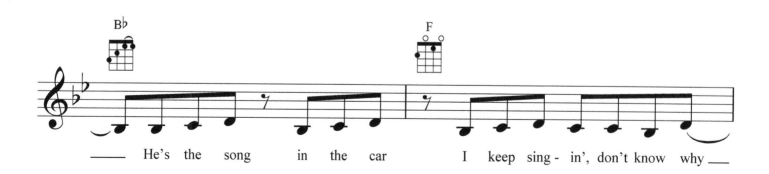

___ He's the song in the car I keep sing - in', don't know why ___

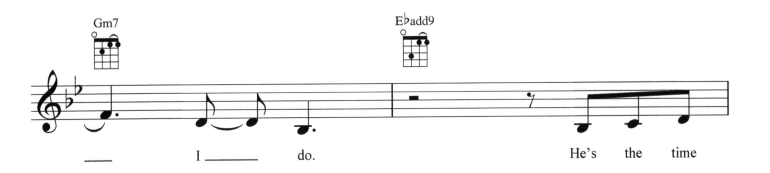

I _____ do. He's the time

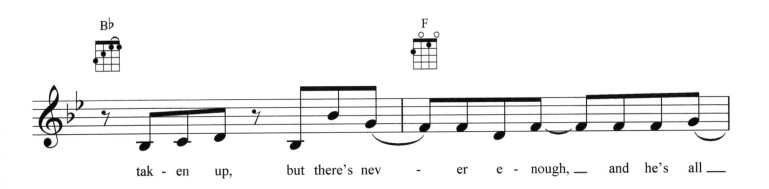

tak - en up, but there's nev - er e - nough, _____ and he's all _____

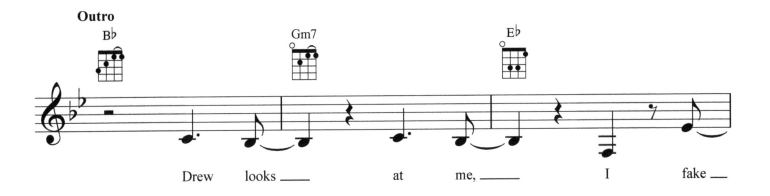

_____ that I need to fall in - to. _____

**Outro**

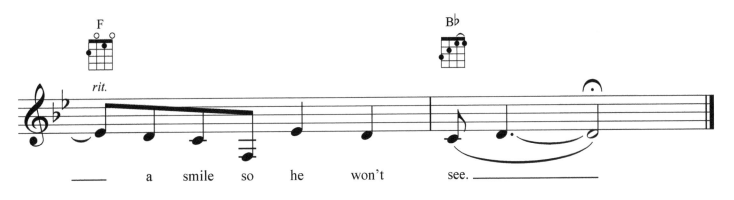

Drew looks _____ at me, _____ I fake _____

a smile so he won't see. _____

# HAL•LEONARD®
# UKULELE PLAY-ALONG

**AUDIO ACCESS INCLUDED**

**1. POP HITS**
00701451 Book/CD Pack...............$14.99

**2. UKE CLASSICS**
00701452 Book/CD Pack...............$12.99

**3. HAWAIIAN FAVORITES**
00701453 Book/CD Pack...............$12.99

**4. CHILDREN'S SONGS**
00701454 Book/CD Pack...............$12.99

**5. CHRISTMAS SONGS**
00701696 Book/CD Pack...............$12.99

**6. LENNON & MCCARTNEY**
00701723 Book/CD Pack...............$12.99

**7. DISNEY FAVORITES**
00701724 Book/CD Pack...............$12.99

**8. CHART HITS**
00701745 Book/CD Pack...............$14.99

**9. THE SOUND OF MUSIC**
00701784 Book/CD Pack...............$12.99

**10. MOTOWN**
00701964 Book/CD Pack...............$12.99

**11. CHRISTMAS STRUMMING**
00702458 Book/CD Pack...............$12.99

**12. BLUEGRASS FAVORITES**
00702584 Book/CD Pack...............$12.99

**13. UKULELE SONGS**
00702599 Book/CD Pack...............$12.99

**14. JOHNNY CASH**
00702615 Book/CD Pack...............$14.99

**15. COUNTRY CLASSICS**
00702834 Book/CD Pack...............$12.99

**16. STANDARDS**
00702835 Book/CD Pack...............$12.99

**17. POP STANDARDS**
00702836 Book/CD Pack...............$12.99

**18. IRISH SONGS**
00703086 Book/CD Pack...............$12.99

**19. BLUES STANDARDS**
00703087 Book/CD Pack...............$12.99

**20. FOLK POP ROCK**
00703088 Book/CD Pack...............$12.99

**21. HAWAIIAN CLASSICS**
00703097 Book/CD Pack...............$12.99

**22. ISLAND SONGS**
00703098 Book/CD Pack...............$12.99

**23. TAYLOR SWIFT – 2ND EDITION**
00221966 Book/Online Audio .........$16.99

**24. WINTER WONDERLAND**
00101871 Book/CD Pack...............$12.99

**25. GREEN DAY**
00110398 Book/CD Pack...............$14.99

**26. BOB MARLEY**
00110399 Book/CD Pack...............$14.99

**27. TIN PAN ALLEY**
00116358 Book/CD Pack...............$12.99

**28. STEVIE WONDER**
00116736 Book/CD Pack...............$14.99

**29. OVER THE RAINBOW & OTHER FAVORITES**
00117076 Book/CD Pack...............$14.99

**30. ACOUSTIC SONGS**
00122336 Book/CD Pack...............$14.99

**31. JASON MRAZ**
00124166 Book/CD Pack...............$14.99

**32. TOP DOWNLOADS**
00127507 Book/CD Pack...............$14.99

**33. CLASSICAL THEMES**
00127892 Book/Online Audio .........$14.99

**34. CHRISTMAS HITS**
00128602 Book/CD Pack...............$14.99

**35. SONGS FOR BEGINNERS**
00129009 Book/Online Audio .........$14.99

**36. ELVIS PRESLEY HAWAII**
00138199 Book/CD Pack...............$14.99

**39. GYPSY JAZZ**
00146559 Book/Online Audio .........$14.99

**40. TODAY'S HITS**
00160845 Book/Online Audio .........$14.99

Prices, contents, and availability subject to change without notice.

# HAL•LEONARD®
www.halleonard.com

0117